Original title:
Hopping Through Dreamland

Copyright © 2024 Creative Arts Management OÜ
All rights reserved.

Author: Lucas Harrington
ISBN HARDBACK: 978-9916-90-492-3
ISBN PAPERBACK: 978-9916-90-493-0

Jumps in the Garden of Enchantment

In the garden bright with blooms,
Children laugh and chase the tunes.
Butterflies dance on petals fair,
Magic whispers fill the air.

Beneath the trees, the secrets lie,
Underneath the azure sky.
Every jump, a dream takes flight,
In the garden of pure delight.

The Mirage of Merriment

Laughter echoes in the breeze,
Moments captured, hearts at ease.
Colors swirl like dreams unfurled,
In the mirage, joy is twirled.

Glimmering like a distant star,
Merriment feels never far.
With every smile, the world aligns,
In this mirage, pure love shines.

Flutters of Night-Time Bliss

Stars above in velvet night,
Whispers soft, a gentle light.
Flutters dance on silken air,
In this bliss, worry's rare.

Moonlight kisses the earth below,
While dreams begin to softly flow.
In sweet slumber, hearts take flight,
Flutters of pure, sweet delight.

A Lark in the Whispers of Time

A lark sings sweet at break of dawn,
Softly waking the world, reborn.
Whispers echo, tales unfold,
In the stories of the bold.

Each note carries a memory,
In the dance of history.
Time flows gently, a river wide,
With the lark as our guide.

The Mirthful Voyage of a Dreamer

In a boat made of wishes, I sail,
With the stars as my compass, I find my trail.
Waves of laughter, the wind's gentle kiss,
Each ripple a secret, a dream to reminisce.

Past islands of wonder, where colors collide,
The horizon, a canvas, where fantasies ride.
Though storms may approach, my heart will stay true,
For the voyage of dreaming is all I pursue.

With crew made of echoes from stories long told,
We chase after moments, both timid and bold.
The sea speaks in riddles, yet I understand,
With a sprinkle of magic and joy from the land.

So I sail through the night, on this mirthful spree,
Every wave, every sigh, a new possibility.
Hold fast to the laughter, let your spirit soar,
For the voyage of dreaming is forevermore.

Echoes of the Waking Night

In the quiet hours, where shadows blend,
The night whispers secrets, our thoughts to mend.
Beneath the soft glow of a silvered sky,
Echoes of the day reflect as they fly.

Each sigh of the breeze holds stories untold,
Of stars that have fallen, of dreams turned to gold.
In the tapestry woven of silence and sound,
The heart finds its rhythm, its peace to abound.

With the moon as my lantern, I wander the street,
Tracing the footsteps where night and day meet.
Voices like murmurs, they linger and fade,
In echoes of twilight, a serenade made.

As slumber draws near, I cradle the night,
In the echoes, I find my calm, my delight.
With the dawn will come shadows of worries untied,
But in echoes of night, my spirit will hide.

Bouncing Between Realms

In twilight's glow, we leap and bound,
Between the worlds, where dreams are found.
Floating on whispers, we chase the light,
In every heartbeat, we take flight.

Colors blend as we spin and sway,
Time loses meaning, night turns to day.
With every jump, we break the seam,
Bouncing boldly from dream to dream.

Whispers of a Velvet Sky

Beneath the veil of a deep, dark blue,
Stars shimmer softly, a cosmic view.
Gentle winds carry tales untold,
Whispers of night, precious and bold.

In the hush of dusk, secrets arise,
Glimmers of hope in the vast, wide skies.
Each twinkle's a promise, a wish set free,
In the velvet embrace, just you and me.

Leaping on Moonbeams

On silver strands that weave the night,
We leap with laughter, pure delight.
Dancing on fringes of shadows cast,
Moments like these are meant to last.

With every bound, the world feels new,
Soft glow surrounds, a shimmering hue.
We glide through dreams, light as a sigh,
Leaping joyfully, you and I.

Dance of the Starlit Shadows

In the glow of the moon, shadows sway,
An elegant dance, night turns to day.
Stars wink above, a celestial cheer,
Echoes of laughter fill the air here.

With every turn, the universe spins,
A ballet of light where love begins.
Together we twirl, lost in the sound,
In starlit shadows, our hearts unbound.

Boundless Imaginings

In whispered dreams, we weave the night,
Ideas take flight, a wondrous sight.
Colors swirl, a canvas bright,
Hearts ignite with pure delight.

In realms unseen, our spirits soar,
Adventure calls from distant shore.
Each thought a key to open door,
With boundless dreams, forevermore.

Celestial Flights

Above the clouds, our dreams collide,
Stars like lanterns, bright and wide.
Through cosmic waves, we boldly glide,
On whispered winds, our hopes abide.

Galaxies dance in timeless grace,
Wonders of space, a vast embrace.
In moonlit beams, we find our place,
Among the stars, we drift and chase.

The Bounds of Slumber's Dance

In twilight's grace, we softly sway,
Through shadows deep, where night holds sway.
Each whispered dream, a gentle play,
In slumber's arms, we drift away.

Beneath the stars, our spirits twine,
With every heartbeat, shadows shine.
In soft repose, our fates align,
In dreams, we find the pure divine.

Moonlit Jaunts Through Enchanted Woods

Beneath the moon, the pathways glow,
Whispers of magic softly flow.
Through ancient trees, where secrets grow,
In twilight's charm, our hearts bestow.

With every step, the night unfolds,
Tales of wonder, softly told.
In nature's realm, our spirits bold,
In moonlit woods, we break the mold.

Flitting Among Ethereal Delights

In gardens where the fairies play,
We dance through mist at close of day.
With laughter bright, we chase the gray,
In ethereal light, we find our way.

Each petal's grace, a fleeting dream,
In harmony, we drift and beam.
Among delights, our spirits gleam,
In whispered joy, we softly scream.

Skimming the Surface of Wishes

Wishes float like petals down,
Dancing softly, kissed by sound.
Fleeting dreams on gentle waves,
A quiet heart, the night it saves.

Starlit skies invite the glance,
Every twinkle sparks a chance.
Rippling hopes in moonlit streams,
Chasing ever after dreams.

In the hush of whispered thoughts,
Every yearning, carefully sought.
Tender moments brush the skin,
A silent promise deep within.

Like shadows shifting in the light,
We find ourselves lost in flight.
Skimming surfaces of desire,
Hearts ignited, set on fire.

Traces of the Enchanted Night

Moonlight drips from ancient trees,
Whispers dance upon the breeze.
Stars, like secrets, softly glow,
Guiding paths where dreamers go.

Each step leaves a trace of grace,
In the stillness, find your place.
Echoes waltz on silver streams,
Carrying the weight of dreams.

Night unfolds a velvet shroud,
Drawing in the curious crowd.
A tapestry of wishes sewn,
In the magic that we've known.

As the hours stretch and fade,
Traces linger, softly laid.
Enchanted moments slip away,
Yet their essence always stays.

Breezes that Tickle the Imagination

Breezes wander through the trees,
Tickling thoughts like playful bees.
They carry whispers, light and free,
Opening doors to whimsy's key.

Gentle gusts that tease the mind,
A world of wonders intertwined.
Each rustle sings a secret tune,
Awakening the heart's balloon.

Sketch the clouds upon the sky,
Let your thoughts take wing and fly.
With every breath of playful air,
Imagination's journey, rare.

So dance with shadows, leap and sway,
Embrace the magic of the day.
For breezes come to lift you high,
To sail on dreams and touch the sky.

The Playgrounds of Shimmering Light

In the dawn, where colors blend,
Playgrounds greet the light, my friend.
Each ray a brush upon the ground,
Crafting joy in every sound.

Children laugh, and spirits soar,
Infinite games, forevermore.
Each shimmer sparkles, bright and bold,
Stories waiting to be told.

Slides of sun, swings of delight,
Chasing shadows, hearts take flight.
In these spaces, time stands still,
With every moment, dreams fulfill.

As twilight drapes its velvet cloak,
New adventures softly stoke.
In twilight's embrace, we embrace the night,
In playgrounds filled with shimmering light.

The Carnival of Sleepythoughts

In a world where dreams collide,
The whispers of night softly glide.
A circus of shadows begins to dance,
As sleep takes hold in a timeless trance.

Bright colors swirl in the moonlight's glow,
With giggles and laughter that gently flow.
Each thought a performer in whims of air,
As wishes take flight without a care.

Round and round, the carousel spins,
In this realm where night always wins.
The heart finds joy in the still and the deep,
In the vibrant show at the Carnival of Sleep.

So close your eyes and breathe in the night,
Let go of the world, embrace the light.
For in this carnival's exquisite grace,
You'll find your dreams in a warm embrace.

Riddles in Midnight's Embrace

Under the stars where secrets dwell,
Whispers unravel each mystical spell.
A dance of shadows, a flicker of light,
In midnight's embrace, the riddles take flight.

Questions hang softly in the cool night air,
Wrapped in the magic that lingers there.
Stars like lanterns wink in delight,
Inviting the daring to ponder the night.

Each riddle unfolds like a petal's caress,
Entwined in the tales that time can compress.
Find joy in the puzzle, the twist in the plot,
For in every challenge, wonder is caught.

So ponder away under the vast, deep sky,
Let your mind wander, let your thoughts fly.
In midnight's embrace where each moment ignites,
Riddles reveal their shimmering lights.

Twists and Turns of Reverie

In the garden of dreams where visions play,
Twists and turns lead the heart away.
Paths of imagination wind through the night,
Each corner a spark of ethereal light.

A tapestry woven of wishes and fears,
Colors that shimmer in laughter and tears.
Every step taken, a chance to explore,
In the twists of reverie, there's always more.

Butterflies flutter with stories to share,
While echoes of wonder drift softly in air.
With every inhale, an adventure begins,
As the soul dances where the true magic spins.

So lose yourself in this wondrous maze,
Let your spirit soar through the twilight haze.
For in twists and turns of dreams that enchant,
Lie the echoes of joy that forever will chant.

Luminous Pathways of Joy

Follow the path where the sunlight gleams,
Luminous trails that awaken our dreams.
With every step, let the heart sing free,
On pathways of joy, just you and me.

Through meadows of laughter, we'll dance and twirl,
Embracing the wonders of this vibrant world.
Each moment a treasure, each breath a delight,
As we wander together in the soft evening light.

The sky painted golden, the horizon aglow,
Inviting our spirits to flourish and grow.
With laughter as music and love as our guide,
In luminous pathways, we'll joyfully glide.

So let's chase the sun and the moon's gentle glow,
For in this sweet journey, blissful seeds sow.
In luminous pathways where happiness flows,
Together we'll journey, wherever life goes.

Surging through Fantastical Streams

In a realm where rivers gleam,
Whispers of the night do dream,
Colors dance beneath the moon,
Flowing fast like a bright tune.

Waves of magic sweep the shore,
Carrying tales of yore,
Beneath the skies, a tapestry,
Of hidden realms, wild and free.

In the current, secrets swirl,
Echoes of a timeless pearl,
Together, we embrace the flow,
Where wondrous currents gently go.

Adventures Unfurled in the Ether

Above the clouds, where dreams take flight,
Stars are lanterns in the night,
Galaxies twirl, a grand ballet,
Guiding our hearts along the way.

Through cosmic seas, we sail with glee,
Boundless realms for you and me,
Charting courses, a wild spree,
Into the unknown, endlessly.

Ethereal winds whisper my name,
Inviting us to join the game,
With every leap, a new surprise,
In this bright space, our spirits rise.

Yonder Where Wishes Flourish

In gardens lush, where wishes grow,
Blossoms bloom in vibrant glow,
Each petal sings of dreams embraced,
In the sun's warm, sweetened taste.

Breezes carry hopes anew,
Painting skies in every hue,
Joyful laughter fills the air,
Echoes of our hearts laid bare.

Yonder paths where wishes weave,
Hold the magic we believe,
Each step forward, joy's cascade,
In the realm where dreams are made.

Leapfrogging Between Worlds

With a hop, we cross the line,
To lands where time does intertwine,
Frogs of fate, we leap with grace,
Finding magic in this place.

Step by step, the worlds unfold,
Stories lost and tales retold,
In every jump, a brand new fate,
Adventures waiting at the gate.

Between the realms, we bounce and play,
Chasing light through night and day,
Explore the gaps, the dreams that call,
Together we will dare to fall.

Echoes of a Starlit Bounce

Whispers of the night unfold,
Beneath the stars, stories told.
Soft glimmers dance on silver streams,
Echoing the heart's wild dreams.

Moonlight drapes the world in lace,
One can find a tranquil space.
With every pulse of cosmic glow,
A rhythm felt, a gentle flow.

The shadows waltz with endless grace,
In secret nooks, dreams interlace.
Each beat a promise, every sigh,
A melody that lifts us high.

In starlit realms, we come alive,
To the echoes, hopes thrive.
With every bounce, the spirits rise,
In the hush of night, we realize.

Prancing Over Dreamscapes

Leaps of joy in pastel skies,
With every twirl, the spirit flies.
Painting clouds in shades of bliss,
Each fleeting moment, not to miss.

Footsteps dance on fields of light,
Guided softly through the night.
Chasing shadows, playful glee,
In this place, we feel so free.

Skimming past the edges bright,
Every heartbeat, pure delight.
In laughter's tune, we prance and sway,
Lost in dreams, we drift away.

Together in this magic land,
With love and hope, we take a stand.
Embracing all that life can give,
In every step, we learn to live.

Waking in a Velvet Sky

At dawn's first light, the world awakes,
A tapestry that sunlight makes.
With velvet hues, the heavens glow,
A gentle kiss, a soft hello.

Clouds drift by like thoughts unspun,
In quiet grace, a day begun.
The breeze carries whispers anew,
Of dreams washed bright by morning's dew.

Mountains stand tall in regal stance,
As nature beckons us to dance.
In the calm, our worries fade,
In this haven, hopes are laid.

Each moment crafted, pure and true,
With every heartbeat, life feels new.
In velvet skies, our spirits soar,
Together finding evermore.

Tumbles Through the Dreamer's Garden

In a garden where wishes bloom,
With fragrant air, dispelling gloom.
Petals whisper secrets sweet,
As daydreams weave in soft retreat.

Tumbles down the winding path,
Chasing echoes of quiet laughs.
Each blossom tells a tale of old,
Of adventures in colors bold.

Butterflies flutter, bright and rare,
In this haven, floating in the air.
With every turn, the heart takes flight,
Into realms of pure delight.

With nature's brush, the world awakes,
Painting dreams the spirit takes.
In this garden, we find our peace,
As joyous blooms bring sweet release.

The Waves of Slumber's Symphony

Soft whispers weave through dreams,
As twilight's curtain gently falls.
The ocean hums a lullaby,
In night's embrace, the world enthralls.

Stars twinkle like distant lanterns,
Guiding thoughts to shores unknown.
Each wave a sigh, a secret told,
In slumber's arms, we drift alone.

Moonlight dances on the sea,
Painting silver paths of light.
With every crest and ebbing flow,
We sail through realms of endless night.

Let the waves rock us to sleep,
In symphonies, we find our peace.
For in the depths of dreams we dive,
Where worries fade and sorrows cease.

Sprightly Spirits of the Moonlit Vale

In the vale where shadows play,
Sprightly spirits leap and twirl.
Beneath the moon's soft silver gaze,
They dance in joy, their laughter whirls.

Whispers wind through ancient trees,
Carrying secrets of the night.
Fleeting flickers of delight,
In sparkling dreams, their spirits breeze.

Fireflies join the dance so bright,
Illuminating paths of hope.
Together they weave a tapestry,
Of wishes spun with every stroke.

Join the revel, lose your cares,
Let the magic fill your soul.
In the moonlit vale, we find our parts,
As sprightly spirits make us whole.

Frolicking in the Realm of Wishes

In fields where wishes bloom and grow,
We frolic under skies so wide.
Each step a hope, each laugh a dream,
In this realm, our hearts abide.

Cotton clouds float overhead,
Carrying thoughts of grand designs.
With every whisper, wishes soar,
To places unknown, like winding vines.

The breeze is filled with fragrant cheer,
As blossoms dance in pure delight.
Here in this land of endless wants,
We chase the stars that gleam at night.

Come, let's wander hand in hand,
Through realms where fantasies ignite.
For in this frolicking embrace,
We'll find our light, our true invite.

Bouncing on the Echoes of Night

Bouncing on the echoes of night,
We leap through dreams both wild and free.
The moon's soft glow, our guiding light,
As shadows sway in harmony.

Laughter rings through midnight air,
A symphony of joy and cheer.
With every bounce, our spirits rise,
Dancing close, we conquer fear.

Stars whisper secrets, oh so bright,
As we glide through this cosmic play.
In the rhythm of the dark, we find,
A vibrant peace that lights the way.

Embrace the echoes, shout with glee,
For in this night, we feel alive.
Together we'll unleash our hearts,
And in these echoes, always thrive.

Dreams Carried on Silken Breeze

Whispers of hope float through the air,
Tender desires dance without a care.
Stars gleam softly in the night's embrace,
As wishes take flight, a gentle trace.

Moonlit secrets weave the tapestry,
Carried by winds that sing of what can be.
Each sigh of night holds dreams yet unspun,
Softly unfolding, like threads in the sun.

In gardens where the wildflowers sway,
The heart finds solace, drifting away.
With open arms, we greet the dawn's light,
Embracing the gift of the new bright.

So let us chase dreams on silken streams,
Where laughter ignites the softest of beams.
In the realm of slumber, we shall find,
The treasures that visit the wandering mind.

The Symphony of Twilight Tread

The dusk will hum a soothing tune,
As shadows stretch beneath the moon.
From day to night, the colors blend,
Creating magic that knows no end.

Footsteps soft on the whispering grass,
Where time forgets and memories pass.
A melody danced in the deepening blue,
With echoes of dreams that feel so true.

The stars awake in the tapestry sky,
A silent chorus, they gently sigh.
With every breath, the twilight leads,
Inviting hearts where wonder breeds.

In this moment, all senses align,
To the symphony where spirits entwine.
Let us wander through shadows and light,
For within the twilight, everything's right.

Vaulting Between Light and Shadow

In the hush of dawn, a contrast sings,
As light breaks free on ethereal wings.
With every heartbeat, the world finds its place,
And shadows retreat, revealing grace.

Kaleidoscopes of whispers paint the day,
While the echoes of night begin to sway.
Life is a pendulum, swinging fast,
Between the moments, both present and past.

When twilight falls, the magic ignites,
A dance of colors in magical sights.
With every leap, the soul learns to grow,
In harmony with the ebb and flow.

Vaulting high where dreams unfurl,
Navigating wonders of this vast whirl.
Let the journey of light and shadow guide,
For in each lesson, the heart will reside.

Enchanted Paths of the Imagination

Where thoughts take flight on feathered wings,
Adventures await in the joy it brings.
Through enchanted woods beneath the sun,
Every path leads to stories begun.

With every step, the mind can explore,
Whispers of legends and days of yore.
In realms of magic where wishes play,
The heart ignites to find its way.

Clouds weave dreams in a tapestry grand,
Where hope and wonder go hand in hand.
Through the mist, horizons unfold,
Revealing treasures more precious than gold.

In the embrace of the sweetest of dreams,
Imagination flows like soft, gentle streams.
So let us wander these paths divine,
For in the enchanted, our souls shall shine.

Whispers of a Moonlit Path

Underneath the silver glow,
The shadows stretch and play,
Whispers float upon the breeze,
Guiding wanderers on their way.

A soft tune calls from the night,
Where secrets beg to be found,
Each step leads to hidden dreams,
Echoes in the hallowed ground.

Along the path of shimmering light,
The trees sway in gentle grace,
With every glance, the world transforms,
As enchantment takes its place.

In silence, hearts begin to soar,
Embracing all the night imparts,
The moonlit path will ever hold,
The whispers shared by wandering hearts.

The Bouncing Clouds of Reverie

Fluffy dreams float overhead,
In a dance of soft delight,
Their shapes twist and twirl away,
Chasing echoes of the light.

On wings of laughter, they drift high,
Painting skies with shades of cream,
Each bounce holds a fleeting thought,
A moment caught in waking dream.

Giggles rise with every puffy form,
As the breezes play along,
With each leap, a memory springs,
Making life a swirling song.

Beneath the vault of endless sky,
We reach for clouds, we dare to fly,
In the realm where daydreams roam,
Finding joy, we call it home.

Dances Between the Stars

Twinkling lights in cosmic waltz,
A galaxy's grand embrace,
Stars unbind in brilliant leaps,
Weaving dreams in boundless space.

Glimmers whisper ancient tales,
From places far, yet near,
With every shimmer, worlds awake,
Creating magic woven clear.

In the void, a symphony,
Harmony among the night,
Dancing shadows twirl and spin,
As the universe ignites.

Join the rhythm, lose your cares,
In the silent cosmic sea,
Every heartbeat synchronizes,
In the dance of unity.

Leaps in the Land of Fantasia

Where dreamers roam on stardust paths,
In Fantasia's vibrant glow,
Joy erupts with each new step,
Adventures blossom, dreams bestow.

Mountains made of candy swirl,
Rivers flow with sparkling wine,
In this land of pure delight,
Every sight is truly divine.

Creatures dance in colors bright,
With laughter soft as morning dew,
They leap and bound with golden grace,
Under skies of fiery hue.

In wondrous leaps, we find our spark,
The essence of our wildest dreams,
In Fantasia, where hearts ignite,
Life flows in vibrant streams.

High Fives in the Cosmos

Stars twinkle lightly in the vast night,
Comets blaze trails, a wondrous sight.
Galaxies swirl in a cosmic dance,
A celebration of fate, given chance.

Planets spin tales of timeless lore,
Interstellar hugs that forever soar.
We reach for the heavens, our dreams align,
With every high five, we gently shine.

Nebulas glow in soft pastel hues,
Each spark a reminder of endless muse.
In this grand expanse, we're never alone,
United in spirit, in starlight we've grown.

So raise your hands up to the deep blue,
In the cosmos' embrace, make wishes come true.
Together we laugh, together we fly,
Through the endless wonders, we'll forever high five.

Forgotten Lullabies and Splashing Dreams

Whispers of night drift on the breeze,
Soft lullabies weave through the trees.
In shadows of sleep, dreams come alive,
Floating on waves where memories dive.

Splashing through puddles of shimmering light,
Childhood echoes beckon from the night.
Each song a treasure, a gentle embrace,
In twilight's hug, we find our place.

Forgotten stories float on a sigh,
Dancing with stars that wink from the sky.
Embrace the silence, let the heart scheme,
In the sweet solace, we dare to dream.

So close your eyes and let visions flow,
Through the tapestry of night, let us go.
To lands uncharted, where wonders gleam,
In forgotten lullabies, we splash and dream.

In the Veil of Midnight Whimsy

Under the cloak of the midnight sky,
Whimsy dances with a gentle sigh.
Fireflies twinkle like tiny stars,
Guiding our hearts to magical shores.

Misty dreams curl like smoke from a flame,
Each fleeting thought, a delicate claim.
Echoes of laughter twirl in the dark,
Painting our hopes with a silvery spark.

Beneath the moon's gaze, we spin and sway,
Lost in the rhythm of night's ballet.
With every step, we paint the unseen,
In the veil of whimsy, where souls convene.

So embrace the mystery that night bestows,
Let go of fears as the soft wind blows.
In this twilight realm, where wishes may be,
We'll dance our dreams into eternity.

The Dance of Echoing Dreams

In a realm where whispers softly collide,
Echoes of dreams in the moonlight glide.
Footsteps of hope on a silken trail,
Where fantasies bloom and fear turns pale.

With every heartbeat, a story unfolds,
In a world where the brave find courage bold.
We twirl through shadows, lost in the flow,
Gathering wishes like seeds we sow.

The night sings sweetly of journeys yet known,
Together, we wander through fields overgrown.
In the tapestry woven of stardust and schemes,
We find our freedom in the dance of dreams.

So take my hand, let's weave through the night,
Unlock the magic, set our hearts alight.
In the resonance of life, let our spirits gleam,
Together we soar in the dance of dreams.

The Meadow of Shimmering Hopes

In a meadow where the wildflowers sway,
Dreams take flight in the warm sun's ray.
Colors dance in the gentle breeze,
Whispers of hopes, as soft as leaves.

Glistening dew on the grass so bright,
Embracing the calm of the approaching night.
Each petal a promise, each stem a song,
In this meadow, we always belong.

The laughter of children, sweet and clear,
Echoes of joy for all who are near.
A canvas painted with shades of delight,
Illuminating hearts like stars in the night.

Take a moment, breathe in the air,
Feel the magic, let go of your care.
In the meadow of shimmering dreams,
Life is woven in beautiful seams.

Driftwood Dreams and Stardust Trails

On a shore where the ocean meets the sky,
Driftwood whispers secrets as it passes by.
Each fragment of time bears a story untold,
Woven in grains of sand and gold.

Stardust trails follow the fading sun,
Guiding our steps, two souls become one.
In the twilight glow, magic appears,
Echoing softly through laughter and tears.

Moonlit nights bring the waves' gentle kiss,
Wrapped in the calm of eternal bliss.
Beneath the stars, our dreams take flight,
A dance of the cosmos, radiant and bright.

Together we wander, hand in hand,
Through the echoes of time and the silken sand.
In the stories of driftwood, we find our way,
Carved in the heart of each passing day.

Cascade of Laughter in the Universe

In the vastness where galaxies twirl,
Laughter cascading, in precious pearls.
Stars burst forth with joyous delight,
As echoes of giggles ignite the night.

Planets harmonize in a symphonic dance,
Each joyful heartbeat, a fleeting chance.
Waves of mirth ripple through the skies,
Painting the cosmos with wonder's guise.

Comets race through with tails of glee,
While moons sway gently, a soft melody.
In the art of the universe, laughter reigns,
Binding us all like celestial chains.

Come gather 'round, let your spirits soar,
In the cascade of joy, there's always more.
With every chuckle, we draw near,
In the laughter of stars, we disappear.

The Chasing of Silver Shadows

In twilight's embrace where the silver falls,
Shadows dance lightly, answering calls.
We chase the echoes that whisper and glide,
Fleeting glimpses of dreams that abide.

Moonbeams illuminate paths unforeseen,
Guiding our steps through the tranquil scene.
Every shadow a story, a secret held tight,
Fleeting yet precious in the softest light.

With each step taken, the night unfolds,
Mysteries woven in silver and gold.
In the chase of shadows, we find our way,
Lost in the magic of night turning to day.

So let us wander, hearts open wide,
In the chasing of shadows, let love be our guide.
Embrace the unknown with joy in our hearts,
For in every shadow, a new journey starts.

Sea of Clouds and Gleaming Pearls

In a sky of shifting dreams,
Waves of clouds drift leisurely,
Whispers of the sunlit beams,
Dance like pearls in memory.

Each horizon holds a tale,
Carried on the breezy flight,
Colors mingle, soft and pale,
Painting day to meet the night.

Glimmers spark in twilight's fold,
As the stars begin to play,
Ephemeral treasures bold,
In the sea where shadows sway.

Let the winds weave through your mind,
Through the clouds that softly part,
Find the treasures you will find,
In the gleaming pearl of art.

A Reverie on Rainbow Springs

Across the meadow green and wide,
Water dances with a song,
Crystal drops in colors slide,
Where dreams and laughter both belong.

With each laugh a rainbow grows,
In the splendor of the light,
From the springs, where magic flows,
Hope ignites the day from night.

Each reflection in the stream,
Mirrors joys we hold so dear,
In this gentle, vibrant dream,
Life transforms when we are near.

Let the waters swirl and gleam,
As the world begins to sing,
In this place, again we'll dream,
By the shores of spring's sweet spring.

Finding Joy in Starry Spheres

Out in the night where silence sings,
Stars awaken with a twinkle,
Each one a wish, a hope that clings,
In the cosmos, hearts will sprinkle.

Galaxies swirl in dance so bright,
Creating tales far and wide,
In the vast and endless night,
Every spirit finds its guide.

Beneath the moon's soft, gentle light,
Whispers drift on cosmic winds,
In the heart, a spark ignites,
Where joy is where the soul rescinds.

Find your place in this grand show,
As the universe expands with grace,
Let your inner wonders grow,
In the joy of starry space.

Twilight Trampolines and Cosmic Lullabies

When twilight stretches long and wide,
And colors blend in soft embrace,
We jump on dreams where hopes collide,
In the dusk's whimsical space.

Each bounce ignites the softly sighs,
As night unfolds its velvet hue,
We leap through twinkling lullabies,
In the realm where wishes grew.

Stars above like cotton candy,
Drifting slowly, bright and bold,
In this moment sweet and dandy,
We find the tales yet to be told.

So let us dance 'neath skies of grace,
On twilight trampolines we soar,
To cosmic songs that time can't trace,
In joyful hearts forevermore.

Fluttering into Fantasy

On wings of whispers, dreams take flight,
In realms where shadows dance with light,
The stars above, like lanterns glow,
Guiding the hearts where magic flows.

A tapestry woven of stardust bright,
With every flutter, igniting the night,
In secret gardens where wishes thrive,
The soul awakens, feeling alive.

Through valleys draped in silken mist,
Where echoes of laughter beckon and twist,
A symphony plays in the breeze's hum,
As fantasy calls, we shall succumb.

So let us dance in this vivid trance,
With every heartbeat, we seize the chance,
To flutter into dreams both wild and free,
In the vivid world of fantasy.

Journey through Cloud Castles

Up in the sky where the soft clouds dwell,
We wander through castles, a magical spell,
With each step floating, we rise and we glide,
Through corridors painted with love and pride.

Glimmers of sunlight break through the gray,
As we dance with the breeze, come what may,
A journey of wonder, our hearts intertwined,
In castles of dreams, our spirits aligned.

The towers are dreams, touching the blue,
With secrets and stories wrapped in the hue,
Through windows of hope, we gaze ever wide,
On this journey through clouds, we are side by side.

So come, take my hand, let's float ever high,
In this realm above, where dreams never die,
Together we'll weave the threads of the kind,
In those cloud castles, forever entwined.

Skipping Across Celestial Paths

A light-footed skip through the heavens bright,
On pathways of stars, we dance with delight,
Each twinkling gem a step in our game,
As we trace the cosmos, igniting the flame.

With constellations to guide our flight,
We weave through the dark, embracing the night,
A playground of planets, a celestial sea,
Skipping across realms, just you and me.

Galaxies whirl in a joyous embrace,
As we leap through the void, a timeless space,
With laughter that echoes among the bright spheres,
We'll treasure these moments, beyond all the years.

So gather your courage, take that first leap,
The universe holds what our hearts wish to keep,
Across celestial paths, we'll forever dance,
In the starlit night, we're lost in the trance.

Flight of the Moonlit Rabbit

Under the glow of the soft moonlight,
A rabbit takes flight on this starry night,
With fur like the clouds and eyes full of dreams,
He hops through the realm, or so it seems.

The silver beams cradle him in their glow,
As he bounds over hills where wildflowers grow,
With each little jump, magic fills the air,
In the hush of the night, with nothing to fear.

Through meadows and streams, the rabbit will roam,
In a world that is fleeting, he calls it his home,
Where every star twinkles with stories untold,
In the arms of the night, he feels brave and bold.

So let us join in on this whimsical ride,
As the moonlit rabbit, our dreams will not hide,
With a leap into wonder, we'll dance on the beams,
In the flight of the rabbit, we'll follow our dreams.

Flickers of Cosmic Laughter

Stars twinkle with mirth, a cosmic dance,
Galaxies swirl in a playful trance.
Whispers of comets, trails of delight,
Echo through vastness, a joyous flight.

Nebulas glow, colors burst wide,
Each light a smile, in the universe's stride.
Planets collide with a jolly cheer,
Cosmic jesters, both far and near.

Black holes chuckle, secrets they hide,
Gravity's giggle, the universe's guide.
In the silence of space, laughter still rings,
A symphony drawn from the fabric of things.

Together they spin, in a radiant show,
Flickers of laughter, in the starlight's glow.
The cosmos rejoices, a radiant choir,
With echoes of jokes that never expire.

Gliding on Feathered Thoughts

Thoughts take flight on gentle wings,
Soaring high, where freedom sings.
On currents of dreams, they twist and sway,
Gliding softly through night and day.

Whispers of wisdom on breezes glide,
Carried aloft, where visions reside.
Feathers of intuition brush the skies,
Invisible paths of the heart's replies.

Each flutter a moment, a spark of grace,
In the vastness of mind, they find their place.
Chasing the shadows, they dance and weave,
Crafting the stories that we believe.

Tethered to wonder, they never fall,
Feathered thoughts rising, answering the call.
In the realm of the mind, where dreams take shape,
Together they soar, a boundless escape.

A Journey Across Illusion's Bridge

Veils of illusion, flutter and sway,
Guiding us gently along the way.
Footsteps of wanderers bold and bright,
Crossing the bridge into endless night.

Mirages shimmer, secrets unfurl,
In the dance of the mystic, the fabric twirls.
Dreams intertwine with the threads of fate,
Journeying onward, we contemplate.

What is real in this shadowed space?
Echoes of truths in an intricate chase.
Through the mist, we dare to seek,
The beating heart of the universe's peak.

At the brink, we stand, hands clasp tight,
Illusion's embrace, a guiding light.
Together we leap, into the unknown,
On this bridge, our spirits have grown.

Frolics Under the Sugar Plum Trees

Beneath the trees where the sugar plums sway,
Children laugh and twirl, lost in play.
Petals fall softly, a sweetened embrace,
Each frolic a moment, a joyful trace.

Laughter spills forth like rivers of gold,
Tales of adventure and dreams untold.
With giggles like bells, they dance on the breeze,
Creating a universe under the trees.

From branches above, candy dreams shower,
Colors ignite, each moment a flower.
As dusk draws near, and shadows descend,
The magic continues, hearts never end.

Under the stars, the stories ignite,
Frolics and friendships bind day into night.
With each whispered secret that blossoms anew,
The spirit of joy in each heart shines through.

Secrets of the Ethereal Garden

In twilight's hush, the whispers sigh,
Petals glow beneath the sky.
Secrets bloom in shadows cast,
Time drifts softly, thick and vast.

Moonbeams weave through branches high,
Painting dreams as stars reply.
Each leaf tells tales of love and loss,
In nature's arms, all paths emboss.

A breeze carries a fragrant tale,
Birds enchant with gentle wail.
Every corner, magic seen,
In the garden, we glean serene.

Dancing lights where fairies dwell,
In this haven, all is well.
The night's embrace, a velvet shroud,
Guarding wonders, soft and proud.

Chasing the Liquid Stars

Glide on waves of cosmic streams,
Chasing echoes of distant dreams.
Each star a tale, a glinting spark,
Guides our hearts through the dark.

With every pulse, we rise and fall,
Listening to the universe's call.
Liquid light in the ocean's sway,
Whispers of night, leading the way.

Sailing threads of starlit grace,
In the dance of time and space.
We twirl in the celestial sound,
In every moment, magic found.

With every wish, we mend the seams,
Crafting futures from our dreams.
Chasing the stars, a wondrous flight,
Together we shine, in the night.

A Tapestry of Dreaming Flights

In colors bright, the weavings play,
Crafting moments that drift away.
A tapestry spun from threads of hope,
Where all are free, and dreams elope.

Through fields of gold, our spirits soar,
Each stitch a tale, forevermore.
The fabric hums with laughter's sound,
In every fold, life's joys are found.

Whispers weave through the night's embrace,
Connecting souls in a sacred space.
In this dreamscape, we take our flight,
Guided by love's eternal light.

Clouds unfurl, like stories unfold,
In the tapestry, futures told.
Together we dance, through shadows and gleams,
In this woven world of our dreams.

Floating on Whimsy's Breath

On whims of laughter, we softly glide,
Beneath the clouds, with joy as our guide.
Dancing through the sunlit skies,
In every bubble, a new surprise.

With floating hearts, we chase the breeze,
Among the petals of flowered trees.
Life's gentle magic hovers near,
Whispers of joy, a song to hear.

We drift along on starlit streams,
Every moment crafted from dreams.
In light's embrace, we learn to play,
With whimsy's breath, we find our way.

As night takes hold, the stars align,
In the quiet, our spirits shine.
Floating through the endless night,
In whimsical laughter, we take flight.

Moonbeam Mirth

In the soft glow of the night,
Moonbeams dance with delight,
Whispers of dreams take flight,
Hearts twinkle, oh so bright.

Silver shadows softly play,
Guiding lost souls on their way,
Laughter echoes, bright and gay,
In the magic of the sway.

Stars join in the joyful cheer,
Casting wishes, drawing near,
Moonbeam mirth, so crystal clear,
Filling hearts with hope and cheer.

Skipping Stone Blossoms

By the river's gentle flow,
Skipping stones, a lovely show,
Petals dance in breezes low,
Nature's song, a tender glow.

Blossoms float like whispered dreams,
Rippling waters spark with gleams,
Serenity in sunlit beams,
Life unfolds in graceful themes.

A moment held, a secret shared,
Joyful hearts all unprepared,
In this world, our souls declared,
Nature's love, forever cared.

Whimsy on a Rainbow Path

On a path of colors bright,
Dreamers wander, pure delight,
Every step, a dance of light,
Joy unbound, hearts take flight.

Lollipop trees and candy skies,
Every turn, a sweet surprise,
Giggling clouds, where laughter lies,
Underneath the painted ties.

With each hue, a story spins,
Whispers of where magic begins,
In this place, where joy wins,
Life unfolds, as it begins.

Floating Through the Midnight Blossom

In the hush of midnight's grace,
Blossoms drift in a soft embrace,
Floating dreams, a tender chase,
Stars glimmer in their place.

Moonlit petals kiss the night,
Curtains drawn, the world feels right,
Floating through, hearts light as kite,
In the dark, we find our sight.

Whispers carried on the breeze,
Secrets shared with gentle ease,
Blossom's fragrance, sweetest tease,
In the night, our souls find peace.

Cavorting Among Celestial Fireflies

In the evening glow they dance,
Tiny sparks in rhythmic trance.
With laughter soft and light so bright,
They cavort in the heart of night.

Whispers drift on a velvet breeze,
Tickling leaves on slumbering trees.
Each flicker tells a secret tale,
Of dreams and wishes that prevail.

Underneath the cosmic dome,
They guide the wandering spirit home.
In their glow, time stands still,
A moment caught, a heart's deep thrill.

The Twilight Ballet

As sun dips low with a golden sigh,
The sky dons hues that mystify.
Stars begin their delicate rise,
A ballet twirls in the velvet skies.

Moonlit shadows softly dance,
A world awash in a twilight trance.
Gentle hues of pink and blue,
Weaving dreams in twilight's dew.

In this performance, night takes flight,
Glimmers of magic scattered bright.
Each heartbeat sways to the night's sweet song,
The allure of dusk, where we belong.

Echoes of Joy in the Ether

In realms where laughter fills the air,
Echoes swirl without a care.
A melody of boundless cheer,
Resonates for all to hear.

Notes of hope like feathers glide,
Carried on the starry tide.
Whispers of joy, soft and sweet,
In the ether, hearts will meet.

With every heartbeat, love is found,
A symphony of life unbound.
In serene moments, spirits soar,
Echoes of joy forevermore.

A Sojourn on the Cloud Trail

Up among the clouds we sail,
On a whimsical, wind-blown trail.
Each puff a passage, soft and white,
Carrying dreams into the light.

In this realm of gentle grace,
We trace our hopes, a timeless space.
With every step, a story spun,
Underneath the watchful sun.

Floating free in the boundless blue,
We dance in shadows, life anew.
On clouds of wisdom, we unfold,
Our journey's worth in tales retold.

Flight of Celestial Bunnies

In the twilight sky so bright,
Bunnies leap with wings of light.
Through the clouds they dance and play,
Chasing dreams that float away.

Whispers of the moon do call,
As they glide, they never fall.
With each hop, the stars ignite,
A ballet of joy in the night.

Silver trails of stardust gleam,
In their eyes, the universe beams.
Upon the winds of wishes flown,
In this realm, they feel at home.

When dawn arrives, they cease to roam,
But in our hearts, they make their home.
Memories of their flight remain,
In whispered winds, a soft refrain.

Delirious forays into Night's Embrace

Beneath the shadowed willow's sheen,
Whispers murmur, soft and keen.
Wanderers dance in silken dreams,
Unraveling the night's sweet themes.

Moonlit paths weave tales untold,
Where hearts beat wild and spirits bold.
Stars above twinkle with delight,
Echoing laughter through the night.

With every sigh, a mystery sways,
In the arms of night, lost in a haze.
Delirious thoughts entwined in glee,
Sipping fate's nectar, wild and free.

As dawn approaches, dreams take flight,
Leaving echoes in morning's light.
A bittersweet farewell we're faced,
From night's embrace, our souls are graced.

The Garden of Infinite Possibilities

In a realm where colors bloom,
Ideas flourish, banishing gloom.
With petals soft and scents divine,
Each flower tells a tale, a sign.

Rivers of light where thoughts flow wide,
Beneath arches where dreams reside.
Every corner holds a spark,
In this garden, nature's art.

Seeds of hope planted deep in earth,
Nurtured by tales of rebirth.
Here creativity knows no bounds,
In silence, the universe resounds.

Take a breath in this sacred space,
Embrace potential, find your place.
For every step leads to the new,
In the garden, the magic's true.

Pouncing on the Stars of Wonder

In the velvet void, eyes alight,
Curiosity takes its flight.
With playful leaps, they stretch and grow,
Chasing constellations' glow.

Pouncing softly on beams of dreams,
Grasping the light in playful schemes.
Every twinkle, a call to play,
In the cosmos, they dance away.

With laughter that fills the silent space,
They spring forth in joy, a lively chase.
Between the planets, through the streams,
They leap onward, lost in dreams.

In the dance of stars, they find their tune,
A symphony played by the night's moon.
And when the dawn begins to sing,
They softly fade, yet leave their fling.

Soaring over Surreal Meadows

In meadows bright, where colors blend,
Under skies that twist and bend.
Whispers of the wind do sing,
As shadows dance and sunbeams spring.

A canvas wide, with brushstrokes bold,
Stories of enchantment told.
With each flutter, joy takes flight,
In a world that feels so right.

Clouds as pillows, gently drift,
Nature's hand, the perfect gift.
Time slows down in this vast sea,
Hearts unbound, forever free.

Soaring high, the dreams unfold,
In surreal meadows, pure and gold.
Where every sigh turns into art,
A journey written from the heart.

Wandering in a Patchwork Dream

Beneath a quilt of vibrant seams,
I wander softly, lost in dreams.
Each patch a story, stitched with care,
Whimsies hidden everywhere.

The moonlight glows on fields of thread,
Where hopes are whispered, softly said.
I trace the patterns, one by one,
In this realm where thoughts can run.

Butterflies dance on quilted paths,
Echoing forgotten laughs.
With every step, new tales begin,
In a patchwork world, I lose and win.

Wandering through these vibrant hues,
I find the courage to choose my muse.
In the fabric of my dreams so bright,
I stitch my spirit, take my flight.

Jumps over the Rainbow's Edge

A leap of faith, I take the chance,
Over rainbows, I start to dance.
With colors bold, I dive and sway,
In this vivid realm, I find my way.

The arching light calls out my name,
Inviting me to join the game.
As laughter spills from skies above,
I find my home in hues of love.

Each step I take on colors wide,
Brings joy that swells like ocean's tide.
I leap and twirl, a vibrant flight,
In the peace of this endless light.

Jumps over land, through dreams I glide,
With every bound, I feel the tide.
In the spectrum, I break free,
A life of magic, joy, and glee.

Gliding through Lullabies

Softly rising, in the night,
I glide on whispers, pure delight.
Each lullaby a soothing song,
Guiding me where I belong.

The stars above create a glow,
As gentle dreams begin to flow.
In the silence, hearts entwine,
Crafting moments, pure, divine.

From shadows deep, I find my peace,
In lullabies, my fears release.
With every note, a journey starts,
Harmonizing restless hearts.

Gliding through the softest night,
Wrapped in tunes of purest light.
In this melody, I'll soar high,
With dreams that never say goodbye.

Delights of a Star-Sprinkled Glade

In a glade where stars do gleam,
Soft whispers float like a dream,
Moonlit petals sway and sigh,
As night winds weave a lullaby.

Crickets play their gentle tune,
Underneath the watchful moon,
Fireflies dance in playful jest,
In this quiet, glowing nest.

Each shadow glimmers, faint but bright,
In this glade, all feels right,
Nature's peace, a soft embrace,
In the stillness, find your place.

Beneath the sky, all worries cease,
Where the heart can find its peace,
Delights swirl in the twilight air,
In the glade, nothing can compare.

The Giggles of Dream Spirits

In realms where visions softly play,
Dream spirits dance and sway,
With giggles echoing through the night,
Casting sparkles, pure and bright.

They weave tales of joy and cheer,
Filling hearts with magic near,
Through laughter, dreams take flight,
Guiding souls towards the light.

Whispers float on silken streams,
In the land where nothing's as it seems,
Echoes of joy in every breath,
Celebrating life, defeating death.

With each chuckle, darkness fades,
In their presence, hope cascades,
The giggles of spirits intertwined,
In dreams, true magic we find.

A Leap into the Impossible

With eyes wide open, heart set free,
I dream of what's yet to be,
A leap into the great unknown,
Where possibilities have grown.

On the edge of fear and chance,
I find my courage, start to dance,
Embracing risks with every stride,
With faith as my unwavering guide.

The horizon stretches far and wide,
A vast expanse, my spirit's pride,
Each step, a whisper of the brave,
In the depths, I find my wave.

With every leap, I break the mold,
In the stories yet untold,
A journey starts with just one chance,
Into the impossible, I advance.

Chasing Shadows in the Starry Realm

In a realm where shadows glide,
The stars reflect what hearts might hide,
Chasing whispers of the night,
Through the dark, they spark with light.

The past lingers, softly calls,
In this dance where mystery falls,
With every step, secrets unveil,
In the hush, a vibrant trail.

Each shadow holds a story deep,
As dreams and fears begin to seep,
Exploring depths of what may be,
In the stillness, I am free.

Chasing shadows, sweet and rare,
In the vast embrace of air,
With each flicker, life is spun,
In this starry realm, I run.

Skylight Serenades

Under the stars, we softly dream,
Whispers of night, a gentle theme.
Moonlight dances on the serene lake,
Echoes of love, in silence, awake.

A tapestry woven from shadows cast,
Time stands still, our worries past.
Notes of laughter drift through the air,
Together we find a world that's rare.

In the cool breeze, melodies sway,
Holding forever this magical stay.
Each note a promise, a vow we share,
In the night's embrace, we're free from care.

As dawn approaches, we bid goodbye,
Yet in our hearts, this song will lie.
Skylight serenades, forever near,
In every twilight, your voice I hear.

Boundless Journeys of the Night

Through the velvet skies, we take our flight,
Chasing dreams beneath the night.
Stars like gems, their glow so bright,
Guiding our path in silver light.

Whispers of wonders brushed in the air,
Each distant twinkle, a story rare.
The moon as our chariot, we ride so high,
In this vast world, we learn to fly.

Galaxies beckon, horizons unfold,
Secrets of night, the brave and bold.
Every heartbeat, a rhythm divine,
In the boundless journey, your hand in mine.

With every moment, our spirits soar,
Through cosmic wonders, we wander more.
In the tapestry of night so wide,
Together we'll roam, forever our guide.

Flight on Cotton Candy Winds

Floating softly on the breeze's embrace,
Colors swirl in a sweet, gentle chase.
Cotton candy clouds, so fluffy and light,
Carry our laughter into the night.

With every gust, new adventures arise,
Beneath a canvas of pastel skies.
Whispers of joy in each tender gust,
Filling our hearts with unyielding trust.

Winds that giggle like children at play,
Lead us to wonders that glitter and sway.
On a whim, we drift through the skies,
Where imagination and freedom lies.

In the realm where dreams come true,
Cotton candy winds will carry us too.
As we chase sunsets, hand in hand,
In this sweet journey, forever we'll stand.

The Dreamer's Meadow

In a meadow where wishes bloom,
Soft petals fill the air with perfume.
Under the arches of the willow tree,
Silent secrets whispered just for me.

Dancing shadows in the evening light,
Wanderers lost in the charm of night.
Where every blade of grass tells a tale,
Of dreams once dreamed that now set sail.

Butterflies flit through the golden hues,
Carrying hopes on the evening dews.
In this land where time holds its breath,
Every moment is a promise of depth.

As twilight falls, the stars are our guides,
In the dreamer's meadow, our heart resides.
Here in the quiet, our souls intertwine,
In this sacred space, forever we shine.

Starlit Sprints Over Dreamscape Hills

Under the moon's soft glow, we race,
Through valleys where shadows chase.
Winds whisper tales of night,
As stars twinkle in playful flight.

Frolicking over hills, so high,
With laughter that dances in the sky.
The night is young, we are bold,
Chasing dreams, let the stories unfold.

Each step a thrill, each heartbeat sings,
Carried away on enchanted wings.
Over the horizon, our spirits soar,
In this wonderland, we seek for more.

In the silence, we find our way,
Navigating through night and day.
The starlit path, our guiding light,
In this dreamscape, everything feels right.

Through Elysian Fields we Bound

In fields of gold where wildflowers bloom,
Life's melody whispers through the gloom.
Each step we take, a promise glowing,
With every heartbeat, joy is flowing.

Butterflies dance in the gentle breeze,
Nature's laughter brings us to our knees.
With arms outstretched, we embrace the sun,
In Elysian Fields, we are forever young.

The horizon blushes with hues so bright,
Painting our hearts with pure delight.
Together we run, hand in hand,
In this paradise, we make our stand.

Among the blossoms, we find our song,
In this world, where we belong.
Through Elysian Fields, our spirits climb,
Bound by love, transcending time.

A Carousel of Fantasies

Round and round, the colors spin,
Underneath the vibrant din.
Horses leap in a joyful dance,
Inviting us to take a chance.

Every turn, a new delight,
Carving paths in the dim twilight.
Wonders weave through the air so sweet,
As dreams awaken and hearts skip a beat.

With painted wings, we float up high,
Embracing the magic as we fly.
A tapestry of stories shared,
In this carousel, we're unprepared.

Through laughter, through tears, we find our way,
In this enchanted land where we play.
Life's fantasies swirl in a dazzling blaze,
In the carousel's charm, we're lost in a haze.

The Waltz of Whirled Wonder

In a twilight embrace, we begin to sway,
The world around us fades away.
With every turn, we spin and twirl,
In the waltz of wonder, hearts unfurl.

Stars adorn the velvet night,
Guiding our journey with their light.
As shadows mingle, time stands still,
In this dance, we find our will.

Floating through realms of imagination,
Lost in a sweet, shared sensation.
With every beat, the universe sings,
In this moment, we are kings and queens.

As dawn approaches, our dance must end,
But in our hearts, the magic will blend.
Through the waltz of whirled wonder, we've soared,
In each other's arms, our spirits restored.